Understanding Cryptocurrencies

Understanding Cryptocurrencies

The Money of the Future

Arvind Matharu

BEP BUSINESS EXPERT PRESS

First published in 2019 by
Business Expert Press, LLC
222 East 46th Street, New York, NY 10017
www.businessexpertpress.com

ISBN-13: 978-1-94858-065-6 (paperback)
ISBN-13: 978-1-94858-066-3 (e-book)

Business Expert Press Finance and Financial Management Collection

Collection ISSN: 2331-0049 (print)
Collection ISSN: 2331-0057 (electronic)

Cover and interior design by Exeter Premedia Services Private Ltd., Chennai, India

First edition: 2019

10 9 8 7 6 5 4 3 2 1

Printed in the United States of America.

Abstract

The book intends to provide a high level overview of cryptocurrencies to a new enthusiast by using layman language and limiting many of the technical aspects, providing a very condensed version of this vast development of digital currencies.

Blockchain is the new revolution after the Internet that is going to change how we do business today. Cryptocurrencies are the money of the future. These two statements are a positive affirmation from many corners around the world. The author provides a balance of introduction and depth regarding blockchain, hot cryptocurrencies, and their comparisons.

Bitcoin, being the pioneer, is discussed in greater detail. The reader will gain the basic idea of bitcoin mining, trading, and investing. With special interest in the various usages of blockchain and interest on traditional banking systems are also discussed.

Keywords

bitcoin; blockchain; borderless currency; cryptography; decentralized technology; digital ledger; ethererum; impact on traditional banking system; increasing acceptance of digital currencies by online businesses; leading cryptocurrencies and their comparison; money of the future; peer-to-peer participation; proof-of-work

Contents

CHAPTER 1

Introduction to Cryptocurrency

What Is Cryptocurrency?

Cryptocurrency is the money of the future. In the current digital era, digital money was already overdue, which makes the arrival of cryptocurrency during the past 9 years as no surprise. Cryptocurrency is a digital or virtual currency that is still in its embryonic stage and has been gaining lots of attention worldwide. It has not replaced the government-issued money yet due to various factors inherent to it. However, the technological advances are filling the gaps and overcoming the current obstacles slowly and steadily.

Remember when the plastic money, that is, credit cards were introduced? Everyone would have thought that time that how a plastic card may be used instead of paper currency. And today, it is unimaginable for a common person to be without credit cards. The initial resistance was overcome by taking care of challenges related to plastic money. On that note, the day is not far when cryptocurrency may remove the need of banks.

The reasons for the attention gained by cryptocurrencies during the past 10 years are multifold. First, it does not exist in a tangible or physical form. It is not a government-issued currency printable on paper. Cryptography is used to ensure its attributes to be used as a currency by which a cryptocurrency can be used as a medium of exchange and perform monetary transactions, in the same way as the printable bills can be used. Cryptography is the science by which intelligible data or information can be scrambled or concealed by using encryption techniques. Encryption is done from the sender side to make the intelligible data into an unintelligible one. Whereas, on the receiver side, the decryption takes place to bring the encrypted data back into an intelligible form again. The processes of encryption and decryption take place via an algorithm. An algorithm stands for a set of instructions in the world of computing. These instructions in a computer programming language perform a specific task.

Cryptocompare.com depicts the process of cryptography in the following diagram:

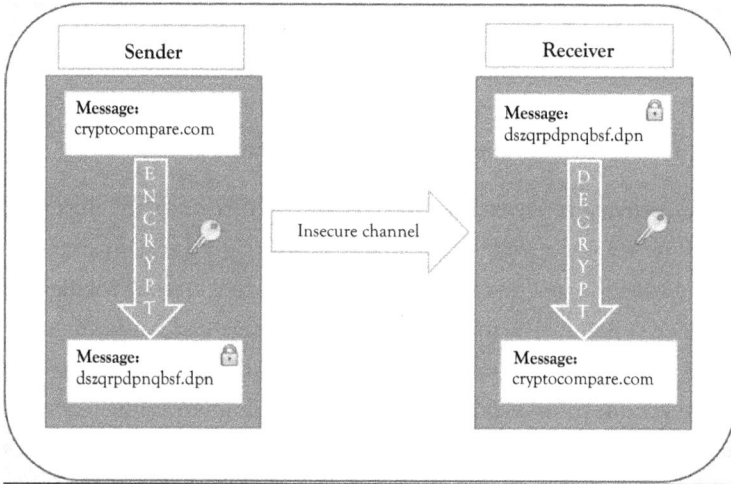

Cryptocurrency derives its name from two words, namely, cryptography and currency; a digital currency controlled by cryptography. A cryptocurrency has no inherent value; however, its value comes from the people's belief in it.

Definitions and Attributes of Cryptocurrency

The Merriam-Webster dictionary defines cryptocurrency as follows:

any form of currency that only exists digitally, that usually has no central issuing or regulating authority but instead uses a decentralized system to record transactions and manage the issuance of new units, and that relies on cryptography to prevent counterfeiting and fraudulent transactions.

The definition from online Oxford dictionary is as follows:

A digital currency in which encryption techniques are used to regulate the generation of units of currency and verify the transfer of funds, operating independently of a central bank.

From these two definitions, the following conclusions can be drawn:

1. Cryptography manages the cryptocurrency by using encryption and decryption techniques.
2. Cryptocurrency is a digital asset that can be used in place of a printable currency toward monetary transactions.
3. There is no central issuing or regulating authority.
4. A decentralized method is used to verify, record, and monitor all the transactions.
5. The decentralized system manages the issuance of new units; those are generally limited in number by the governing algorithm.

Considering cryptocurrency has no central or regulating authority; its value is defined by consensus from people believing in it. It is a borderless currency with which international payments can be made cheaper than conventional currencies. A conventional currency such as a U.S. dollar is governed by a central bank that defines its value represented by printable bills, coins, drafts, cheques, or other similar banking instruments. The value of cryptocurrency comes from an encrypted code that is difficult to reproduce, making it scarce and limiting its numbers, unless the creator of cryptocurrency decides to change the underlying algorithm to create more units. Being a bank-free or border-free currency, cryptocurrency offers an alternative to conventional currencies.

The basic unit of a cryptocurrency is called a coin that is an encrypted code consisting of a string of characters. A coin is merely an entry in a database available publicly via a blockchain that can be called as a distributed ledger.

A blockchain validates the coins of cryptocurrency. A blockchain is certainly a revolution that is here how we are going to see the world in the coming decades. The blockchain is already in the process of making its place as something much bigger than the Internet itself.

What Are Its Origins?

Bitcoin is generally accepted as the first cryptocurrency that came in the form of open-source code in 2009. As the source code is openly available, there are thousands of variants of the original bitcoin available today. Such variants are also called alternative coins (altcoins) that stand for alternative digital currencies.

In October 2008, Satoshi Nakamoto published a paper titled *Bitcoin: A Peer-to-Peer Electronic Cash System*. The identity of Satoshi Nakamoto is still unknown, whether Satoshi is an individual or a group of individuals. In this white paper, Satoshi Nakamoto created and developed bitcoin's original reference implementation. Using the blockchain database, Satoshi released the very first bitcoins in January 2009. Satoshi mined the genesis block of bitcoin, also known as block 0 (zero). Mining is a process by which individuals verify and record the transactions. This set of transactions is called a block, which gets added on top of the past blocks. Altogether, this chain of blocks (of transactions) is known as a blockchain. Miners doing mining are rewarded for their efforts. It is interesting to know that the genesis block had a reward of 50 bitcoins. The genesis block has a timestamp of 18:15:05 GMT on January 3, 2009.

As words such as cryptocurrency, blockchain, bitcoin, and mining will be commonly used throughout this book, these topics will be dealt in more detail in the upcoming chapters.

Why Is It Important to Know About Cryptocurrency?

Cryptocurrencies have seen a significant growth in 2017. There have been wild swings in their value, making these very risky and volatile, due to which these get labeled as a bubble as well. It is very unpredictable when the price continues to rise, and then falls suddenly, only to come back with a newer peak, and so on. People look at cryptocurrencies with various perspectives. Some look at it to perform actual monetary transactions. Some look at it as miners to get rewarded. Some look at it as an investment where retail and institutional investors continue to increase with time. Lot new interest from various other perspectives make cryptocurrency a very interesting digital asset.

What Is the Legal Status of Cryptocurrencies?

The legal status of cryptocurrencies is under radar by most of the countries. The stand varies from country to country. Though their usage may not be illegal and can be used as a medium of exchange in some countries, some countries have taken a hard step to ban or restrict. Countries such as Bolivia, Ecuador, India, Nigeria have declared public statements declaring such restrictions.

Bitcoin being the most popular one, the U.S. Treasury classified it as a convertible virtual currency, and taxed it as a property. Governments worldwide are taking steps to include the transactions using cryptocurrencies into their taxation system.

Is This Not Used for Anonymous Transactions for Illegal Purposes?

The dark side of cryptocurrencies is related to the common notion that these are used for illegal activities, especially on the Dark Web. This leads to continuous rise in the price of the coins. It is unfortunate that more than a quarter of bitcoin usage is linked with criminal activities due to its anonymity. It is important to understand that, just because cryptocurrencies are used by criminals, it should not lead to the conclusion of making cryptocurrency illegal. With the technological advances, and appropriate legislations and controls, it can be better used as a valid and reliable form of currency, making it the future of the money.

CHAPTER 2

Blockchain Is the New Revolution After the Internet

What Is a Blockchain?

The blockchain is the brainchild of Satoshi Nakamoto as referenced in Chapter 1. Satoshi used two separate words, block and chain. With time, the two words have combined into a single word blockchain. Originally, blockchain was devised for bitcoin (cryptocurrency), but it has evolved much bigger since then. A blockchain can be viewed as a publicly available digital ledger that contains a record of the transactions. This kind of database is accessible to anyone, and there is no centralized version of it. In other words, a blockchain is a decentralized technology. It is important to understand that the blockchain technology is not necessarily for financial transactions only, and it can be used wherever any uniqueness of records is required.

A blockchain is presented by Blockgeeks.com in the diagram shown on page 8.

The users of the network participate in the blockchain. This user-to-user (peer-to-peer) participation makes the blockchain centralized. This kind of recordkeeping can be extended to any business domain. The full potential of application of the blockchain technology is still under investigation. The most attractive part of the blockchain is removal of the intermediary party between two users. Currently, finances and identity management are on the top of the applications of a blockchain.

The white paper by Satoshi refers to blockchain as follows:

> ...system based on cryptographic proof instead of trust, allowing any two willing parties to transact directly with each other without the need for a trusted third party...

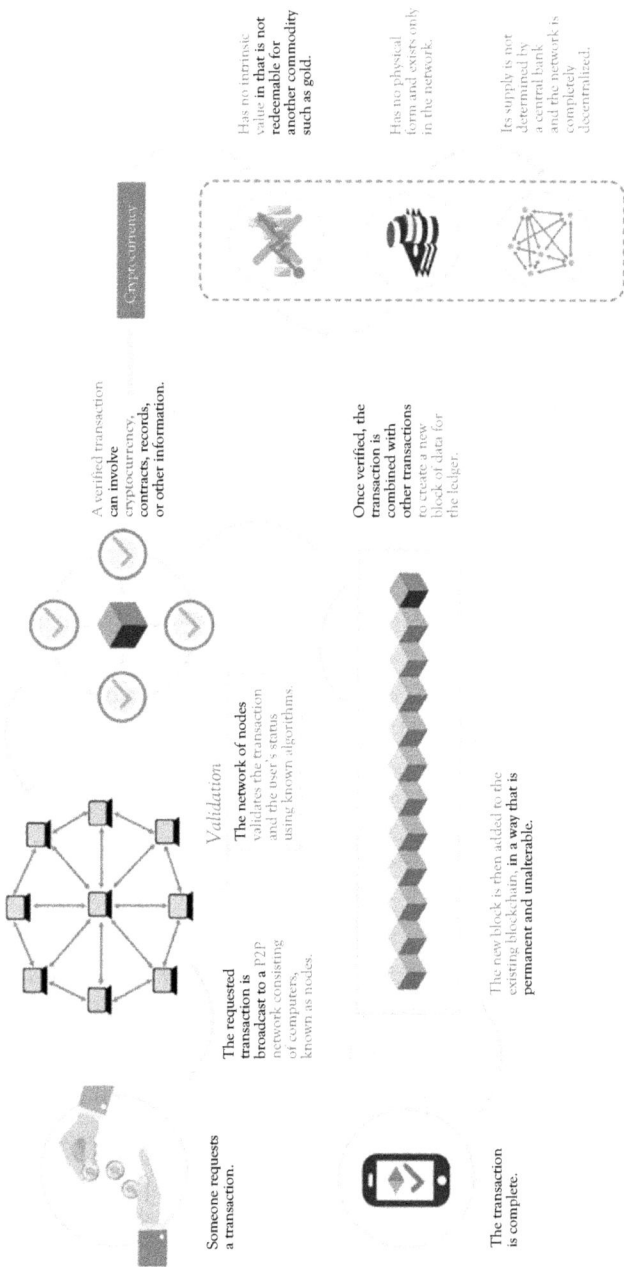

Cryptocurrency

Has no intrinsic value in that is not redeemable for another commodity such as gold.

Has no physical form and exists only in the network.

Its supply is not determined by a central bank and the network is completely decentralized.

Someone requests a transaction.

The requested transaction is broadcast to a P2P network consisting of computers, known as nodes.

Validation

The network of nodes validates the transaction and the user's status using known algorithms.

A verified transaction can involve cryptocurrency, contracts, records, or other information.

Once verified, the transaction is combined with other transactions to create a new block of data for the ledger.

The new block is then added to the existing blockchain, in a way that is permanent and unalterable.

The transaction is complete.

Currently, most of the systems on the Internet require a third party that blockchain tends to eliminate altogether. This elimination of third-party intermediaries is certainly a threat to the conventional (and expensive) methods.

Accordingly, a blockchain can be considered to have the following attributes:

1. Consider this as a digital ledger available publicly.
2. Records in this shared ledger use encryption and decryption.
3. Timestamped creation, validation, verification, and monitoring of the transactions in a decentralized manner.

It should be noted that a blockchain does not have to exist publicly. In that case, the nodes exist in a private network with access to the distributed ledger. A blockchain is a continuously growing list of records, called blocks, linked using cryptography. A block contains a group or batch of valid transactions. A block in the blockchain has the cryptographic hash of the previous block in the blockchain. A cryptographic hash is equivalent to a digital fingerprint. This linking of the adjacent blocks forming the chain resists the modification of the data contained within the blockchain. The authentication of the records takes place with the mass collaboration by the users. This makes the blockchain a secure database where the records become almost unalterable. Conventional centralized databases have their own challenges related to data integrity and security at very high costs to the businesses that get eliminated with the use of the blockchain technology.

The data integrity of the records is an iterative process tracing back to the genesis block. Consider the genesis block as the very first block of the blockchain, also called as block 0. As mentioned earlier, cryptocurrencies are based on the open-source code that anyone may update to create newer digital currencies. A genesis block is generally hardcoded in the software, that is, already present in the base software. This is the only time, where the genesis block is not linked with any previous block via cryptographic hashes. A blockchain can be visualized as a vertical stack that is ever growing with new blocks, where every new block is back-linked with the previous one. The first block is base of this vertical stack.

The latest block is called the top block. The distance between two blocks is called height.

Structure of a Blockchain

A blockchain is a chain of blocks, where a block contains a batch of transactions. A block also contains a header. The transactions are organized in a hash tree along with the hash of the root in the header. A hash tree or Merkle tree in cryptography is a hash-based data structure that is a generalization of the hash list. A Merkle tree is a tree structure in which each leaf node is a hash of a block of data, and each non-leaf node is a hash of its children. In a binary tree, a node is a leaf node if both the left and right child nodes of it are null.

Researchers Wei Cai and Victor Leung of the University of British Columbia present the blockchain structure in a simple diagram as follows:

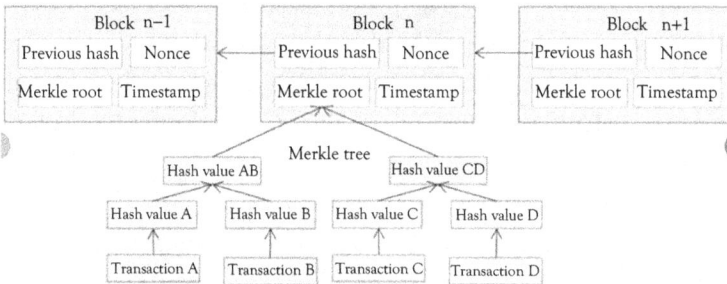

Merkle trees are efficient due to hashes, where hashes can be viewed as ways of encoding files that are much smaller than the actual file itself. In a Merkle tree, each node has up to two children, technically known as branching factor of two. These trees facilitate efficient and secure verification of very large data structures.

How Is a Blockchain Linked to Cryptocurrencies?

A blockchain is to cryptocurrencies, what the Internet is to an e-mail. An e-mail can be sent using the Internet, though the Internet can be used for many more other purposes as well. Similarly, cryptocurrencies are built on the blockchain technology, whereas a blockchain can perform things much more than handling cryptocurrencies. The details of such usages are covered in the chapter where use cases are elaborated.

All cryptocurrencies are blockchains, but all blockchains are not cryptocurrencies. Both blockchain and cryptocurrency go hand in hand. A blockchain can be extended to anything of value, and not currency only. Blockchain is a technology, whereas cryptocurrency is an asset. Bitcoin being the first application of blockchain, the two terms bitcoin and blockchain got used inadvertently for quite some time. However, blockchain has evolved much bigger than just supporting cryptocurrencies only.

A cryptocurrency is a digital token used for a monetary transaction between two individuals. A number of nodes validate the transaction without involving any expensive third-party intermediaries. The nodes have their individual copy of the distributed ledger where various users verify whether the token is double spent or not. Also, the balance is published after the users have verified the transaction. The updated ledger gets published every 10 minutes for bitcoin. This update includes the consensus-based batch of transactions in the form of a block on top of the current tree. The users worldwide must agree to the legitimacy of the transaction. Once a block gets added to the blockchain, the balances get updated permanently.

The blockchain relies on the computer processing power of the network. The users within this network update the distributed ledger and secure the blockchain. That is why, it is important to have a variety of users worldwide. Generally speaking, a healthy blockchain exists if one group of users or an organization does not own more than 51 percent of the computers on the network. Ownership more than this potentially may lead to stop transactions, hence making the blockchain ineffective.

Technological Overview of a Blockchain

A blockchain is a chain of back-linked blocks, with each block containing a batch of transactions, where the number of transactions are set by the underlying protocol. A network of participating computers called nodes continue to add and store blocks in this blockchain. These nodes verify the transactions before adding these to the block. The nodes also solve the underlying complex mathematical problem. After these two activities, the block gets added to the blockchain with reference to the previous block.

Encryption and decryption are used for the security of the data. A mathematical formula is used to hide data using encryption, whereas decryption is used to bring the hidden data back into its original form. A blockchain uses cryptographic hashing to achieve this. The mathematical formula used to encrypt the data related to the transaction along with metadata produces the output called hash. This hash can be viewed as compact information regarding data. With the help of set of keys, the same hash gets produced.

The public key and private key play a significant role between the two users (of a transaction). The public key, as the name suggests, is available publicly, but the private key is not. The sending party uses the private key to send the data (transaction) in an encrypted form. The nodes use the public key to decrypt the sent data to ensure that there is no double spending. Double spending gains more relevance in digital currencies, as digital information can be reproduced relatively easily, which may be used twice or multiple times. To avoid this problem, the cryptographic protocol called proof-of-work (PoW) is used. This ensures that the digital currency is not used more than once by the user. A blockchain uses the SHA256 PoW function that makes the verification process hard to compute, but easy to verify, to avoid the double-spending problem. On that note, there are many PoW systems.

A cryptographic hash is a signature of the digital data, where the SHA256 function produces a 256-bit, that is, 32-byte signature of the digital data. This generated signature of a fixed length is almost unique, which cannot be decrypted back into the original data. Regardless of small or big data, the SHA256-produced signature has a fixed length always. Based on the theory of probability, there are extremely low chances to have same signature or hash due to 2^{128} possible combinations.

Technically speaking, a hash pointer is used to back-link to the previous block in a blockchain. The hash pointer is a combination of the address of the previous block and the hash of the data within the previous block. This makes the blockchain very secure, as it keeps on building on previous blocks. A block header contains the block version number, current timestamp, computational problem, hash of the previous block, nonce, and hash of the Merkle root. A nonce is an integer between 0 and 4,294,967,296.

Microsoft has presented the block structure as follows:

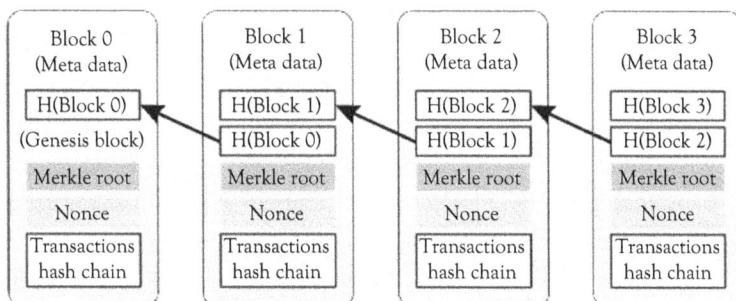

Block 0 (Meta data)	Block 1 (Meta data)	Block 2 (Meta data)	Block 3 (Meta data)
H(Block 0)	H(Block 1)	H(Block 2)	H(Block 3)
(Genesis block)	H(Block 0)	H(Block 1)	H(Block 2)
Merkle root	Merkle root	Merkle root	Merkle root
Nonce	Nonce	Nonce	Nonce
Transactions hash chain	Transactions hash chain	Transactions hash chain	Transactions hash chain

Why Are Users Validating the Transactions?

The users on the network gets rewarded for their collaborative efforts to validate the transactions. The activity of looking for a new potential block to be added to the blockchain is called mining. The users performing the mining process are called miners. The process of mining involves compiling new recent transactions, in the form of a block and solve a comparatively difficult mathematical problem. The miners verify that the new transactions are legitimate. When a transaction gets broadcasted on the network, various miners around the world get on the task of mining. In a way, a competition starts to verify the new transactions to be part of a potential new block and solution to the computational problem. However, a winner is who is able to provide a PoW first, which the block gets added to the blockchain. The winner miner gets rewarded for this effort of mining in the form of cryptocurrency coins. The difficulty of calculating hashes increases with every iteration. This makes the digital currency increasingly scarce similar to printable currency. The underlying algorithm of the cryptocurrency poses a limit on the number of coins, for example, bitcoin can have a maximum of 21 million bitcoins as per the current algorithm.

Why Is Blockchain Gaining So Much Importance?

Many blockchain projects are underway worldwide in what is called Web 3.0. Web 1.0 was the name given to the very first form of *World Wide*

Web. Web 2.0 came up with global sharing of information and social media. Web 3.0 has the decentralization of information at its heart. This is also called human-centered Internet because of the fact that the information is back in the hands of its rightful owners. With decentralization, middle parties are eliminated; those may have monopolized the related business domain with their own selfish motives. Overall, the end user has full control over their data and its security, and not a third party, including government.

Considering the aforementioned benefits of Web 3.0, many applications have started emerging during the past couple of years that are taking away the monopoly of existing widespread applications from big corporations. Brave, Experty, Storj, and Status are some of the examples in Web 3.0 serving the same purpose as Web 2.0 apps browser, video or audio calls, storage media, and messaging perform.

What Are the Other Uses of a Blockchain?

The blockchain technology is much bigger than supporting cryptocurrencies only. As mentioned earlier, a public blockchain is a digital register of records available in a secure and transparent manner, in a decentralized environment without needing any expensive third-party intermediaries. A blockchain is expected to have a great use in a number of fields such as identity management, supply chain management, accounting, voting, stocks, smart contracts. These usages are also referred as use cases. This topic of other uses of a blockchain is dealt with in a greater detail in Chapter 10.

What Are the Hardware or Software Requirements?

The system requirements of a blockchain in terms of hardware and software vary drastically based on the perspective. The perspectives may include those of an end-user, investor, developer developing the blockchain, and company investing in the blockchain project internally or externally. For an end-user or investor, there is no typical requirement, and a normal laptop in current use can be used. Developers need access to the relevant programming language for development. The computation power increases dramatically for the nodes performing mining to produce the PoW. This is required as the increasingly difficult level of computational problem must be solved before the PoW-supported block can be added to the blockchain.

Why Do I Really Need to Know About It?

In the current digital era in the making of Web 3.0, where a blockchain or decentralization is focused on bringing control from the big corporations to the end-user, it is certainly of interest to anyone who would like to see reduced costs of operations while being in a safe and secured environment, where the transactions take place in an efficient and quicker manner.

CHAPTER 3

Hot Cryptocurrencies Around the World

Is Bitcoin the Only Cryptocurrency?

Bitcoin is not the only cryptocurrency. Bitcoins are generated from the open-source code that anyone can modify. The bitcoin inspired many other alternative digital currencies (altcoins) to come in existence, which happened by changing the underlying algorithm. The framework offered by bitcoin still remains at the core for the newer altcoins. These altcoins are similar to bitcoins. Every altcoin has its own blockchain and consensus rules.

Altcoins differ from bitcoins in many ways. Some altcoins offer better privacy, and others may offer lesser privacy. Some offer different proof-of-work functions, while others may not offer any at all. There are many altcoins those have just updated some parameters in the original open free-source code and those may not be that important. Most of the available altcoins today can be called bitcoin clones, where an insignificant parameter such as transactions speed, distribution method, or hashing algorithm are updated, adding not much value to this new altcoin.

In fact, increasing the number of overall coins in an altcoin is similar to effects produced by increasing the printable currency, that is, it becomes readily available, hence becomes lesser in value. The consensus rules and the computational problems to be solved further decide the value of an altcoin. Some people may think that they have missed the wave of a bitcoin, and start investing in some obscure altcoin, that is very risky.

What Are Other Cryptocurrencies?

Currently, there are more than 1,000 altcoins in place. Anyone can create a new altcoin anytime. A bitcoin is the most known digital currency with maximum market capitalization and the largest blockchain. Next to bitcoin are Ethereum, Ripple, Bitcoin Cash, Litecoin, and many more.

It must be noted that the digital currencies have captured market worth more than 250 billion U.S. dollars. This has potential to disrupt the conventional financial world where the government-issued currency is dominant. Decentralization would also mean that the control will not be in the hands of government or big corporations, instead the control will be in the hands of a common person. For survival of big corporations, sooner and later, they have to adopt to the blockchain framework. Even if some countries have banned cryptocurrencies, still its mass adoption in technological giants are making them stronger.

Bitcoin certainly has the advantage of being the first cryptocurrency that is also the most known and widely accepted one. Bitcoin alone has captured market worth more than 100 billion U.S. dollars. The immediate next one is Ethereum with market capitalization of more than 45 billion U.S. dollars. Also, bitcoin has the most value compared to the altcoins. The year 2017 really captured the attention worldwide where the bitcoin price soared super high. For bitcoin value, compare its value of 800 U.S. dollars in January 2017 with approximately 18,000 U.S. dollars in December 2017. That is where bitcoin captured so much attention, and everyone wanted to know about this biggest technological breakthrough after the Internet. No other commodity, including gold or stock, has soared so high in value in so less duration.

The list of other cryptocurrencies called altcoins apart from bitcoin continues to change at a rapid speed based on various factors, including market capitalization. Regardless, Ethereum, Ripple, Litecoin, Dash, NEM continue to be in the top 10 of the list.

Why So Many Cryptocurrencies?

After bitcoin in 2009, Namecoin was the first altcoin produced in 2011. It is interesting to note that, even if more cryptocurrencies may seem not adding value to the world of cryptocurrencies, still these further solidify the idea of decentralization. This allows developers to experiment with more and more features or functions. The bitcoin community may decide to pick up anything useful from those new experiments, making bitcoin innovating, stronger, and secure.

Many altcoins came into existence due to the availability of free open-source code of bitcoin. These altcoins appeared by presenting themselves as better variants of bitcoin that may not be the case in reality. Various cryptocurrencies have declared their own focus as well. Various identified goals are such as smart economy based on digital assets, smart contracts, cheaper international handling of funds, decentralization application platform. All such goals lead to the creation or existence of currently available cryptocurrencies. General market opinion is that such big market capitalization may be based on speculation only, and not necessarily due to the technology factor.

Each cryptocurrency has its own motive. Due to the huge success and presence of bitcoins, other people started their own digital currencies as to become rich quickly. They may have presented almost similar coins, and kept many coins with them in the beginning, with a hope that their coin would get popular and they will hit the jackpot too. Not to forget, even a fraction of market capitalization of bitcoin has the potential of making people millionaires in the quickest way possible.

On the other hand, the altcoin may be really good one, in which the developers are experimenting with new ideas, functions, or parameters. They have far better motives than the ones mentioned in the previous paragraph. Again, there is a hope that those altcoins will get popular one day, and the creators reap the benefit out of those, even if a fraction of those by bitcoin.

Ethereum stands apart from other altcoins, as it focused on fixing the problems with bitcoin. The bitcoin blockchain has already gone so far, that one cannot go back to fix those. On that note, Ethereum has presented smart contracts, and offers Ethereum virtual machines (EVMs). This way, it is much more than an altcoin. Stated correctly, Ethereum offers a decentralized platform to run smart contracts. These offer applications without the need of a complex business logic, downtime, fraud, or third-party interference.

The digital currencies literally exploded in 2017. Also came the concept of initial coin offerings (ICOs). The start-up companies offering new cryptocurrencies raise funds using the ICOs. The venture capitalists have their rigorous process of fund raising that gets bypassed by the ICOs. In short, it is viewed as an unregulated means by the startup venturing into new cryptocurrencies.

Is This a Scam?

Currently, bitcoin investment is very volatile. On that note, investment in the altcoins is even more volatile, making those riskier alternatives. Similar to stocks, big players may invest heavily in some new altcoin, giving an impression that its value will increase more in the coming time. This attracts the people who may think that they missed the bitcoin boat. When this hype works for an altcoin, it brings in money from lots of investors. One fine day, the scammer altcoin disappears after looting this collected money. This makes very important to avoid any such hype and do due diligence on your own. As they say, it is not wise to invest more than what one may afford to lose.

There is a huge rise in new cryptocurrencies after the huge success of bitcoin and other altcoins. With the digital currencies, cryptocurrency exchanges also started rising. Their selling factor is security and transaction fees. Unfortunately, there are not many such exchanges those can be trusted. Many claiming to be solid exchanges disappeared overnight taking the user coins with them. Imagine a bank offering lucrative products to attract a huge number of customers who deposit their assets there. And when millions or billions of funds get deposited in the bank, the bank disappears overnight! And there goes all the deposits by the users who trusted that bank. Unfortunately, some users lost their life savings as well.

Is This a Bubble About to Burst Anytime?

Many analysts worldwide have predicted bitcoin as a bubble and extended that prediction to altcoins as well. This means a prediction of their collapse in the near future. As many as eight Nobel laureates have mentioned bitcoin and altcoins as economic bubbles. A professor even went on to say these as *mother of all bubbles*.

Nobel laureate Robert Shiller defines a bubble as:

a situation in which news of price increases spurs investor enthusiasm, which spreads by psychological contagion from person to person, in the process amplifying stories that might justify the price increases, and bringing in a larger and larger class of investors who, despite doubts about the real value of an investment, are drawn to it partly by envy of others' successes and partly through a gamblers' excitement.

Many experts have criticized cryptocurrencies repeatedly. These have been compared with Ponzi schemes where one gains returns for a short period of time, and the actual owners are benefitted based on the trust and investments by the users. American investor Warren Buffett continues to repeat his stand against bitcoin by calling them non-productive assets.

Regardless, market has seen a great rise in the price of bitcoin and altcoins during 2017, and it has been continuously increasing, though with unpredictable slumps in between. People tend to compare the blockchain with dot-com bubble. During the dot-com period, many people made enormous money, while many more lost huge amounts. Still, it led to a technological evolution on which we stand today. Considering this argument, even if time proves blockchain as a bubble that collapses, still, one must not forget about the revolution it has created in terms of the idea of decentralization and ownership coming back into the hands of end users.

The rapid increase in the number of altcoins and their arbitrarily fluctuating price is a big risk. A user may not understand how a blockchain or altcoins work and may invest in these, which are strongly not advisable, considering the digital currencies are yet to mature.

CHAPTER 4

What Makes Bitcoin So Popular?

What Is a Decentralized System?

Decentralization eliminates the third-party intermediaries and connects two users directly. That is why a decentralized system is also known as user-to-user or peer-to-peer system. Currently, Internet is centralized. The two terms centralization and decentralization are antonyms of each other in terms of a controlling authority. In a decentralized system, no single authority exists to control, and there are multiple points to perform the work as per the prescribed protocol regarding verification, solving of the computation problems, and consensus method.

Facebook and Google are examples of centralized platforms, whereas BitTorrent and Napster offer peer-to-peer file sharing on decentralized platforms. This way, the data is not in the hands of a single party and makes it much more secure comparatively. Synereo has emerged as a new platform for decentralized social networking in comparison to Facebook. The users in this platform can interact with each other directly, without going through a central server. In addition, the data gets encrypted, increasing the security of the transferred data. Even the creators of the platform cannot access this data. Users performing the verification of data get incentive for performing their tasks for the applications in the decentralized platform.

BitTorrent is a good example to understand a decentralized platform. The data does not pass through a single point and passes through multiple points those are part of the peer-to-peer (P2P) network. In BitTorrent, when a user downloads a torrent file, two numbers get listed for the best file download, that is, seeder and leecher. The number of people uploading the file are referred to as seeders, and the leechers stand for the number of people downloading the file. The download process speeds up when the ratio of seeders and leechers is higher. Some websites restrict downloading of contents to the users who do not upload anything.

Any central authority, including governments, interested to control data have more interest in a centralized environment even if it means to have expensive methods in place to do so. On the other hand, a decentralized environment offers much more privacy and security. Facebook and Google are the giants of a centralized environment where any information goes through their servers, and the administrators there have the ability to go through everything going through those. With a decentralized platform, this does not happen, and the end user has the control of their own data eventually.

How Is It a Borderless Currency?

Border in the borderless refers to the geographical borders of countries. Both borderless and borderfree are used interchangeably. Not only a bitcoin can be used as a media of exchange between two users, it is acceptable by many e-commerce-based websites as well. This means that the digital currency can be used for monetary transactions anywhere in the world, not just in the local geographical area. With more and more people getting in the digital currency wagon, more businesses are accepting bitcoin for payment.

Currently, there are hundreds on online businesses accepting digital currencies. Major retailers such as CheapAir, Expedia, Microsoft, Shopify are some of the names in the big list of businesses that accept bitcoin as a payment method for goods purchase. This gives a pleasant feeling that bitcoin is not necessarily for criminal activities. It has already made its way into acceptance by major retailers, hence adding to its legitimacy. The list of such businesses is growing rapidly.

Bitcoin and other altcoins are not only borderless, these are bankless as well. There is no need of a third-party bank to perform the transaction. This significantly reduces the transaction fees due to elimination of overhead costs by the banks. Another major benefit is the reduced transaction time. With bitcoin blockchain updates at an interval of approximately 10 minutes, the transaction time gets reduced from days to minutes. Therefore, a borderless currency like bitcoin can be used to transfer funds around the world without a bank. Certain digital currencies require users to reveal their identification via digital identification, making the users not anonymous anymore. Another interesting development is the debit cards those are able to transact on bitcoin accounts.

Why Is the Bitcoin Price Rising So High?

Bitcoin price leaping to approximately 17,000 U.S. dollars in 2017 has made many early investors millionaires. There are some important factors contributing to the soaring price of bitcoin. The first and foremost factor can be related to the intended legitimacy of the bitcoin by the Wall Street. Social media updates regarding huge injections by big financial institutions result into an expectation that the bitcoin price will continue to rise more. The launching of futures products by CBOE Global Markets and CME Group lets the users to treat bitcoins trade similar to stocks. As per their publication, the Cboe Bitcoin Futures Contract will use the ticker XBT and will equal one bitcoin. The CME Bitcoin Futures Contract will use the ticker BTC and will equal five bitcoins. Such developments indicating acceptance create more confidence in the legitimacy of bitcoin.

Media hype, political uncertainty, and risk are other factors contributing to the rise in the price of bitcoin. Media hype is helpful when people do not use their own brain toward analysis and depend on other users. The thought that, if other person is doing it, and that person is very intelligent, then I also should do it leads to more investment. Media continues to publish about bitcoin, making people feel they should not miss the bitcoin wagon.

Political risks with uncertainty and risk also contribute to the increasing price of bitcoin. In those situations, people tend to transfer money out of their country to safeguard it, before it becomes of no or lesser value. The economic crisis of Greece and Brexit (Britain to leave the European Union) are fine examples of such uncertainties. People became uncertain of their deposits in the local banks there and started transferring it around to save its value. This also impacted positively on the bitcoin price.

Taxation in many countries is still undecided about how to handle bitcoin trading or profits gained from the transactions. One thing is clear that most countries have started realizing that the profits must be treated as done for other currencies, but lack of clear regulations on its use impacts the bitcoin price. The acceptance or rejection of bitcoin by various countries adds or reduces its legitimacy, respectively, hence the rise and fall in the price as well.

Why Is Bitcoin So Volatile?

Volatility is expected to decline as the cryptocurrency grows. The past growth chart of bitcoin has shown sudden surges and dips in its price. As of today, it is a highly unpredictable growth chart. No one can say with confidence where the price will go in the coming future. Where one lobby calls this a bubble, there is totally opposite lobby those who do not hesitate to predict value of one bitcoin to reach 1 million U.S. dollars!

Regarding volatility of the bitcoin price, the cryptocurrency enthusiast terms this part of the process of bitcoin evolution. Compared with global stock markets, global currency, and global gold market, the bitcoin has captured only a fraction of those. These global players have been in market for quite a long time and are stable enough. Whereas the bitcoin is relatively a new entrant, though still with an impressive and unprecedented growth with a huge following already. In short, bitcoin is a junior compared with these (global mature) seniors.

Introduction of new cryptocurrencies that aim at getting rich quickly and flee overnight decrease faith in them for a newcomer. Since the time of government-issued currency during last thousands of years, there is no single global currency. Every country or government has its own variant. Similarly, expecting bitcoin to become a global digital currency is more of an imagination. Altcoins are bound to come up in such a decentralized environment, where monopoly has to go away, and control of own information must come back in the hands of a common man.

Again, media plays a great role in the value perception by the users or would-be users. Bad press induce fears among users. In particular, when Mt. Gox (then a popular bitcoin exchange) declared bankruptcy in early 2014, it created public panic. Also, when FBI investigations revealed bitcoin transactions toward drug dealing, this caused reduced rate of adoption by the users. Further news of security breaches dilute the interest of users. Bitcoin has its own share of security risks; those may appear due to ripples by the security fixes. Such negative press news is bound to create fluctuations, hence the volatility in the bitcoin prices.

The supply and demand theory in economics states that the rarer something is and the more in demand it is, the higher the price will be. Considering there are 21 million bitcoins, there are about 20 percent of the bitcoins yet to be mined as of mid-2018. The mining of 80 percent bitcoins have made the bitcoins scarce. This scarcity has contributed to the rise in the bitcoin price.

One wonders whether bitcoin will ever become stable enough. This is possible with the wider acceptance and confidence in it by the users. More user involvement, decreased transaction time and fees add to the value. Also, taxation and regulation by various governments pave a way toward legitimacy of digital currencies.

Am I Too Late to Invest in It?

"HODL!"

Hodl is an Internet slang term used in the bitcoin community when referring to holding the cryptocurrency, rather than selling it. In a bitcoin forum message, a user incorrectly typed *hodling* in the place of *holding*. Since then, hodling got popular and synonym with staying invested in bitcoin.

Early investors in bitcoin became instant millionaires due to their early adoption. The question about being late in investing in bitcoin got asked at many stages of the bitcoin price say at 1, 10, 1,000, 10,000, or even at the peak of 17,000 U.S. dollars. The bitcoin price growth is very unpredictable. Still, there seem to be investors reaping profits, though those may not be comparable with what is already done during 2017. In short, no one knows if it is too late or not.

As the user confidence continues to increase, government regulations come into place, more retailers continue to accept bitcoin as a media of exchange, market capitalization grows, and then bitcoin is bound to have even more growth than today. At the same time, the absence of these factors can cause adverse effect as well.

Bitcoin may be considered for long-term investment, where one should only put that one can afford to lose, with a hope that the bitcoin price will eventually increase more one day.

CHAPTER 5

Comparison of Various Cryptocurrencies

What Other Cryptocurrencies Are Available?

Based on the free open-source code for bitcoin, thousands of variants are available. Some call themselves better than bitcoin, although that may not be the case. Bitcoin is certainly a trendsetter for other cryptocurrencies. Altcoins have the same framework as that of bitcoin. A few other more-known digital currencies after bitcoin are Bitcoin Cash, Dash, Ethereum, IOTA, Litecoin, Monero, NEM, Ripple, and Zcash. The transaction speed, transaction fee, unit price, active community, acceptance by users and retailers, and so on, are some of the various factors based on which the digital currencies make in the list.

Despite of the many current and upcoming digital currencies, bitcoin is still maintaining a great hold as a leader due to its acceptance, popularity, and market capitalization. Ethereum and Ripple are more accepted by the corporations and have their major backing.

Altcoins try to capture market by presenting themselves with some objective. These objectives are not just financial and penetrate into different business domains as well. Dentacoin is a good example where it is presented as a platform to provide solutions to benefit the users of the dental industry, ranging from dental professionals and patients. It offers an incentive to both the user groups. Dentacoin is built on top of the Ethereum blockchain. Dentacoin (DCN) is not minable, but pre-mined. The total DCN supply is 8 trillion that will be unlocked gradually as per the predefined schedule.

How Did Others Come Up?

Thousands of cryptocurrencies have come up in a couple of years, as those are relatively easy to make from the open-source code by changing some parameters. Further, initial coin offerings (ICOs) appear to be the *get rich quickly* scheme. Most of the market capitalization is based on speculation and acceptance by the main stream. Government regulations, if any, affect the confidence in the digital currency. An experienced software programmer could make an own coin within 30 minutes to one day maximum. However, the step of programming is not considered the first step, if someone is interested to create own coin. There are many more other factors like interest and involvement from the community before taking such steps, instead of creating a coin first and then looking for the interested community.

On that note, such variants of bitcoin those are created by changing some insignificant parameter do not offer any economic or technological advantage to the users. However, a coin that fixes some problems in the original code and offers new functions certainly results into an innovation. Unfortunately, such innovations die a premature death if the user community, including miners, loses interest during its slump time. It is important that the user community stays motivated throughout for the success of an altcoin.

One may ask how many cryptocurrencies we need in the world, for which there is no answer, considering there is no government-issued currency all over the world, which may be called global, though some of those may be dominating and influencing other economies. There are 180 government-issued currencies in the world today.

What Are the Objectives Served by the Leading Cryptocurrencies?

Most of the variants of bitcoin serve the same objective, that is, financial transactions between two users. However, there are others, which present different and interesting objectives to the user community. In a way, it helps enticing the new users who hope to make big money by investing early in those startups.

The following information summarizes the leading cryptocurrencies and their objectives.

Bitcoin

The main objective of the bitcoin was to create digital money. To have a media of exchange without any third party and governing authority. The decentralization brings control back into the hands of the common man, with reduction in the expensive overheads due to banks, and ability to transfer funds internationally. Another feature of bitcoin is the anonymity of its users.

Ethereum

Ethereum is different from bitcoin in terms of a decentralized environment designed to run smart contracts. A smart contract is a computer protocol intended to digitally facilitate, verify, or enforce the negotiation or performance of a contract. Credible transactions can be run without a third party, which are trackable and irreversible. The objective of the smart contracts is to provide security much better than the traditional contract law, with reduced transaction costs. Ethereum presents the idea in the form of building unstoppable applications, that is, with no downtime, censorship, fraud, or third-party interference.

Ethereum apps run on a custom-built blockchain to facilitate moving value around and represent the ownership of the property. Ethereum Foundation is a non-profit Swiss organization contributing toward new innovation toward the Ethereum platform. Ethereum wallet allows the user to hold and secure ether (the basic unit of Ethereum). The wallet allows a user to secure other cryptocurrencies built on the Ethereum platform. Corporations find Ethereum attractive because of its ability to write, deploy, use, and manage smart contracts with increased security and lesser transaction costs.

Solidity is the programming language to write smart contracts. One can design own cryptocurrency or a digital asset of value on the Ethereum platform. For that, one should create a tradable digital token. The tokens use a standard coin function. This enables the contract become compatible with any wallet or contract. One can fix the total number of tokens in the beginning. These tokens do not have to be fixed, considering the coded software can have certain rules set to change the number. Other uses of Ethereum include kickstarting a project with a trustless crowdsale, to start an organization, transparent voting process, or to build a new kind of decentralized application.

Ether is the crypto-fuel for the Ethereum network that is used to operate the distributed application platform Ethereum. Visualize ether as a form of payment, or incentive to the developers, to ensure that useful productive code of high quality is written, keeping the network healthy. The supply of ether is finite. During the 2014 presale, the gathered donations decided the total amount of supply of ether and its rate of issuance.

Ethereum.org states the results of this presale as follows:

- In total, 60 million ether created to the contributors of the presale.
- About 12 million (20 percent of the preceding) were created to the development fund, most of it going to the early contributors and developers and the remaining to the Ethereum Foundation.
- Ethers are created every block (roughly 15 seconds) to the miner of the block.
- About 2–3 ethers are sometimes sent to another miner if they were also able to find a solution, but this block was not included (called uncle/aunt reward).

Ether and bitcoin do not serve the same purpose. Ether is more of incentive to the developers, and not intended to be used as a currency or asset. As mentioned earlier, it is a crypto-fuel to keep the network running. Wallets exist to perform an automatic conversion of ether and bitcoin.

Ripple

Ripple presents itself as the world's only enterprise blockchain solution for global payments. As per ripple.com, it compares its RippleNet solution with conventional payments solutions those are projected as slow, unreliable, and expensive. Ripple captures the market by connecting banks, payment providers, digital asset exchanges, and corporates. This is achieved via RippleNet to provide one frictionless experience to send money globally.

Ripple is a real-time global settlement network offering instant, certain, and low-cost international payments. Ripple is different from bitcoin and other altcoins in the sense that it does not need mining. Ripple has been integrated into the payment networks of a handful of global banks, with a market capitalization of more than 1 billion U.S. dollars in 2017. Ripple offers various solutions such as xCurrent, xRapid, and xVia to process payments, source liquidity, and to send payments, respectively.

With Ripple, banks are able to tap into new opportunities. RippleNet processes international payments in real time with end-to-end tracking and certainty. The bank benefits with new revenue, lower costs, consistent experience, and one integration point. For payment providers, RippleNet offers increased payment volume, one integration for greater reach, and transparent predictable payments. Corporates benefit from RippleNet from payment tracking, delivery confirmation, capital efficiency, and significant improvement over data reconciliation. Digital asset exchanges attract global payments volume and benefits from the new and reliable volume with faster settlement.

Ripple is a privately owned company that makes it not decentralized enough, as there is company's control over the system.

Bitcoin Cash

In mid-2017, a group of developers prepared a code change in the original bitcoin code. This change also known as a *hard fork* resulted into splitting of the original bitcoin blockchain. Any one owning bitcoin at the time of this hard fork also got possession of the same number of bitcoin cash units. The reason of this hard fork was a want to increase the blocksize. This want was not taken well by the user community, as the original source code was well maintained with a widely accepted set of rules. However, when the code change got in place, this hard fork resulted into this spin-off of bitcoin. This was mainly due to the failure to agree on the best approach by the leaders of the bitcoin user community regarding bitcoin's global growth and presence.

Litecoin

Litecoin was among the first of the cryptocurrencies after bitcoin. It offers a global payment network without any central governing authority. Litecoin has faster block generation rate that means a faster transaction confirmation. Litecoin.com states that litecoin is fully compatible with the bitcoin API. This means that litecoin can be easily integrated into existing applications supporting bitcoin. Litecoin's faster confirmation makes it more suitable for small purchases. Goods and services can be bought with litecoin similar to bitcoin.

Dash

As per Dash.org, Dash stands for digital cash. Dash can be used for instant and private payments online or in-store. One needs Dash wallet to do so. Payments are confirmed in less than a second. It protects one's financial information in terms of the activity history and balances. The Dash website states regarding security—Transactions are confirmed by 200 TerraHash of X11 ASIC computing power and over 4,500 servers hosted around the world.

Dash has features in addition to those of bitcoin that speed up the payment processing. A small group of people decide the future of Dash, making it not decentralized enough. Dash was originally known as Dark-coin. It offers more anonymity making transactions almost untraceable.

EOS

EOS offers the infrastructure for decentralized applications. EOS has gained attention because of its ability to raise more than 1 billion U.S. dollars via initial coin offerings. The focus of EOS is future development of blockchain technologies. As per the ios.io site, EOSIO is software that introduces a blockchain architecture designed to enable vertical and horizontal scaling of decentralized applications.

NEM

NEM cryptocurrency attracts users based on its consensus mechanism and supernode program. The result of this is an open public blockchain that can grow without ever compromising the throughput or stability (Ref: nem.io). The NEM Smart Asset System allows one to customize how to use the NEM blockchain. The NEM technology allows multiple ledgers to coexist on one blockchain. The NEM blocktime is one minute.

Stellar

Stellar is known as an open-source protocol for value exchange. The business objective of Stellar cryptocurrency is to move money across borders quickly, reliably, and for fractions of a penny. Stellar.org states that it is a platform that connects banks, payments systems, and people. It expands access to low-cost financial services to fight poverty and maximize individual potential (Ref: Stellar.org).

Cardano

Similar to bitcoin, Cardano is a decentralized public blockchain and cryptocurrency project. As per cardano.org, Cardano is developing a smart contract platform that seeks to deliver more advanced features than any other existing protocol. Cardano is home to the Ada cryptocurrency that can be used to send and receive digital funds. Cardano states itself more than just a cryptocurrency and calls itself a technological platform with a capability of running financial applications. The layer-based development allows system flexibility in terms of maintenance.

Tronix

Tronix (TRX) is the official currency of TRON, which aims to be a decentralized entertainment content-sharing platform. The tron.network website presents the users the benefits of high throughput, scalability, and high reliability. The Tron website explains how these benefits are materialized. High throughput is achieved by improving the transactions per second (TPS) in TRON. TPS wise, it has surpassed bitcoin and

Ethereum. TRX consistently handles 2,000 TPS, 24 × 7, whereas TPS is 25 for Ethereum and 3–6 for bitcoin.

Tether

Tether provides benefits of both the open blockchain technology and traditional currency. It converts cash into digital currency. The Tether platform is built on top of the open blockchain technologies. Every tether is backed 1–1, meaning that every tether dollar is equivalent to the government-issued dollar. Tether.to publishes the reserve holdings on a daily basis, subject to professional audits.

Binance

Binance is a combination of two words, binary and finance. Binance issued its own token called binance coin (BNB) from the initial coin offerings. The official website binance.com states that BNB runs natively on the Ethereum blockchain and follows the ERC20 token standard. The token was established with a total supply of 200 million. BNB can be used to pay for trading fees on the exchange. BNB has a discount and repurchasing plan in place to attract users. BNB plans to build a decentralized exchange, with BNB as one of the key assets and incentive.

VeChain

VeChain has its cryptocurrency VET, is a blockchain platform with a focus on financial services, supply chain management, and smart contracts. VET pioneered to partner with Chinese government and created a disaster recovery plan. VeChain is a blockchain platform for products and information. By leveraging on the blockchain technology, VeChain strives to build a trust-free and distributed business ecosystem, which is self-circulating and scalable. VeChain offers the API gateway service, third-party services, and distributed data storage. VeChain has implemented blockchain solutions across various industries such as luxury goods, liquor, and agriculture. It has deployed 111 nodes around the world (Ref: verchain.com).

Project PAI

The focus of Project PAI is on PAI, that is, personal artificial intelligence. As per the white paper on projectpai.com, it presents a utility network coin for using PAI, a 3D intelligent avatar designed to look, speak, and behave like a human being in the digital space. This is directly owned and managed by the original user. The user gets compensated for doing so. The PAI network is a decentralized platform and digital avatar repository to interact with decentralized applications.

The white paper defines a digital profile as any form of personal identifier that can be contributed to the creation or improvement of PAI. Some examples include: biometric, voice capture, facial recognition, semantics, social activity, and even personality.

Huobi Token

Huobi exchange is a leading cryptocurrency exchange by volume. Huobi exchange has created its own cryptocurrency Huobi Token (HT) similar to Binance (BNB). HT enables voting for coin listing, as well as being rewarded for doing so. Huobi offers subscription schemes in five tiers.

0x

0x (ZRX) is an open protocol for decentralized exchanges on the Ethereum blockchain. As per 0xproject.com, in the 0x protocol, orders are transported off-chain, massively reducing gas costs and eliminating blockchain bloat. Relayers help broadcast orders and collect a fee each time they facilitate a trade. Anyone can build a relayer. Benefits of 0x are trustless exchange, shared liquidity, and open source. It is built on Ethereum's distributed network with no centralized point of failure and no downtime; each trade is settled atomically and without counterparty risk. The 0x protocol is a pluggable building block for dApps that require the exchange functionality. The goal of the 0x project is to address the inefficiencies of decentralized cryptocurrency exchanges, as well as the inability of various exchanges to work together.

Ethereum Classic

As per ethereumclassic.org, Ethereum Classic (ETC) is a smarter block-chain; it is a network, community, and cryptocurrency that takes digital assets further. In addition to allowing people to send value to each other, ETC allows for complex contracts that operate autonomously and cannot be modified or censored.

This may be best explained with an analogy, imagine bitcoin as a landline phone—it does one thing very well. ETC is like a smartphone—it can do everything bitcoin can and much more (Ref: ethereumclassic.org).

NEO

NEO is a blockchain platform and cryptocurrency designed to build a scalable network of decentralized applications. NEO presents itself as an open network for smart economy.

As per Neo.org, it is a non-profit community-based blockchain project that utilizes the blockchain technology and digital identity to digitize assets, to automate the management of digital assets using smart contracts, and to realize a *smart economy* with a distributed network.

NEO uses a delegated Byzantine Fault Tolerance (dBFT) consensus mechanism and can support up to 10,000 TPS.

Neo.org further states its vision of the future in the following terms:

- Digital assets are programmable assets that exist in the form of electronic data. With the blockchain technology, digitization of assets can be decentralized, trustful, traceable, highly transparent, and free of intermediaries. On the NEO blockchain, users are able to register, trade, and circulate multiple types of assets. Proving the connection between digital and physical assets is possible through digital identity. Assets registered through a validated digital identity are protected by law.
- Digital identity refers to the identity information of individuals, organizations, and other entities that exist in the electronic form. The more mature digital identity system is based on the PKI (public key infrastructure) X.509 standard.

In NEO, we will implement a set of X.509-compatible digital identity standards. This set of digital identity standards, in addition to a compatible X.509 level certificate issuance model, will also support the Web of Trust point-to-point certificate issuance model.

The NeoContract smart contract system is the biggest feature of the seamless integration of the existing developer ecosystem. Developers do not need to learn a new programming language, but can use C#, Java, and other mainstream programming languages in their familiar IDE environments (Visual Studio, Eclipse, etc.) for smart contract development, debugging, and compilation. NEO's Universal Lightweight Virtual Machine (NeoVM) has the advantages of high certainty, high concurrency, and high scalability. The NeoContract smart contract system will allow millions of developers around the world to quickly carry out the development of smart contracts. NeoContract will have a separate white paper describing the implementation details.

IOTA

IOTA is a protocol that achieves consensus on the state of matters in a network. Iota.org states its vision to enable all connected devices through verification of truth and transactional settlements that incentivize devices to make available its properties and data in real time. This gives birth to entirely new general-purpose applications and value chains.

Monero

Monero is a decentralized cryptocurrency. It attracts users with its security, privacy, and untraceability. Monero is a secure digital cash operated by a network of users. Similar to bitcoin, the transactions are verified by consensus. Once transaction gets recorded on the blockchain, it can be reversed.

Zcash

Zcash targets to provide enhanced privacy to users. Similar to bitcoin, the transactions are published on a public blockchain. Zcash offers users an ability to hide sender or receiver information via an optional privacy feature. It has fixed 21 million units in total as bitcoin has.

What Makes Them Different From Each Other?

Cryptocurrencies discussed so far are different from each other in many ways. Most of the virtual currencies are copies of bitcoin with some changes in insignificant parameters, in an effort to look different from bitcoin. This is in the hope that users will show confidence in that digital currency one day, and the owners or users possessing those coin can make money out of that.

Ethereum evolves the game by bringing the Ethereum virtual machine. Similarly, other cryptocurrencies attract various communities with their unique objectives or focus on particular entity or business domain.

Which One Is Better?

Considering the acceptance, popularity, security, privacy, and market capitalization, bitcoin is certainly standing as the leader of all the cryptocurrencies. Ethereum with its presence with smart contracts is the immediate next one.

The aforementioned are just my opinions only, as there is no way to predict which way these two may go in the future.

If Bitcoin Is Already Gone So Wildly High, Should I Consider Investing in Other Cryptocurrencies?

One must not invest what they cannot afford to lose. There is no harm in becoming the early investors of another promising cryptocurrency that shows good user acceptance and confidence, and an active community supporting. Bitcoin took nine years to reach this level, which is actually not a very big duration. Remember a developer used 10,000 bitcoins to buy two pizzas in 2010. Considering the current value, the developer would have been a multimillionaire today.

CHAPTER 6

How to Get Started on Bitcoin

Get Started on Bitcoin

The exponential growth of bitcoin in 2017 and emerging of numerous altcoins caught attention of people worldwide. If you have set your mind on bitcoin, then the upcoming chapters will provide more information about it from various perspectives such as end user, miner, investor, trader, or may be creator of another altcoin.

What Are the Various Methods to Own Bitcoins?

Various methods to own bitcoins is via buying, exchanging, or mining.

The most straightforward method to own bitcoins is via bitcoin exchange. Users can buy or sell bitcoins from the bitcoin exchanges using their local currency. Coinbase is one of the well-known digital currency exchanges to do so. One requires a coinbase wallet to perform these actions. Not only bitcoin, one can exchange other cryptocurrencies, including bitcoin cash, Ethereum, litecoin, and many more via this exchange using local currencies. A user can use their banks or credit cards to buy bitcoins. The exchanges have their stringent criteria for the verification of the users. The exchange services are not available in all countries, or may have partial services available where it is.

Another way is to look for people or agencies selling bitcoins. One must be extra careful in a way similar to conventional shopping. Localbitcoins.com allows filtering based on criteria, such as city, where one may decide to buy from. Local sellers willing to sell their bitcoins for cash or other cryptocurrencies are there. Various payment methods allowed are bank transfers, PayPal, MoneyGram, and so on.

Amazon accepts bitcoins as a payment method. If one owns an online store, then the goods or services can be sold in the same way. Many online retailers, including Amazon, eBay, allow a user to open their own store there, where they charge a fees for listing or selling items. The seller can start owning bitcoins by accepting bitcoins as the payment method for the goods or services offered. The seller needs to spread the word about accepting bitcoins as the payment method. Also, the seller needs a bitcoin payment processing service with which they will be able to convert bitcoins into dollars.

Technical people may choose to become miners. Miners participate in the verification process of transactions for a block, along with solving a computational problem, before a consensus method leads to the addition of that block on top of the previous block in the blockchain. Mining is not an easy job. Bitcoin has gone way ahead in the game, where a single person or desktop is not enough to perform mining due to gigantic computing power required. Mining for bitcoin at this stage does not appear to be a good idea. It certainly used to be a great thing to do in its early days of mining. Bitcoin incentive of mining continues to decrease. Even if the bitcoin value is way too high or may increase even higher, still the hardware and software required to performing bitcoin mining today does seem to be way too expensive to do so. One may look for another cryptocurrencies that are still in their starting phase, hoping that they will become as lucrative as bitcoin has.

Where to Store These?

Digital wallet is used to store bitcoins. Remember, bitcoin is a digital asset. There is no physical coin. Bitcoin address is a public key that can be shared with others. Wallet stores the private key, and not the actual bitcoin. A wallet is able to store several private keys. Generally, a wallet refers to an online location, though cold storage may also exists in the form of a physical USB drive, or paper, and so on.

Different types of wallets can be classified as electronic or cloud based, software based, hardware based, paper based, and mobile based. Another type of classification is hot or cold. An online wallet is called hot, and the offline wallet is called cold.

Online or cloud-based wallets are provided on the Internet. One should be on the Internet to access these. Coinbase is one such provider that is most well-known with a huge consumer base.

Hardware-based wallets are USB-like devices with a screen. The side buttons help navigation through the contents on screen. These wallets allow the user to allow more than one cryptocurrency in terms of private keys and public addresses. These can also be plugged to a laptop to view the contents. Trezor and Ledger are two leading companies that manufacture hardware wallets.

Paper-based wallets are what the name suggests. User prints the private keys and public addresses on a paper for storage. This is possible for bitcoin and some altcoins as not every cryptocurrency offers this. One can use these paper wallets for bitcoin transfers.

The process to obtain a paper-based wallet is a little bit technical, but worth it due to its safety, if the user takes extra precaution for its safety. For this, while being connected to the Internet, a user visits bitaddress.org and saves the webpage on a local drive. After locating the webpage, the user should disconnect from the Internet. A user can now open the webpage in a browser. The opened webpage shows a degree of randomness. When the mouse is hovered over the contents randomly, the degree of randomness changes. The user must get this number to 100 percent that produces the bitcoin address and a private key for printing on a piece of paper. It is always good to keep a backup copy of the private key and save in a safe location. The paper wallet needs same attention for the storage as other valuables in a safety deposit box. If a user leaves or refreshes the site, or generates a new address there, then the recent contents get lost, and a new pair gets generated, making the previous key not retrievable. The private key is like a password to a user account, hence should not be shared. Sharing of the private key may lead to access to all the bitcoins associated with that address. The user needs to provide this bitcoin address to other users to receive bitcoins from them. At blockchain.info, a user can check the balance or spend bitcoins there.

Cryptocurrencies have their own desktop wallet that can be installed on the desktop or laptop. Generally, users prefer to have a desktop wallet, instead of storing their bitcoins or other cryptocurrencies on the exchanges.

Mobile wallets are the applications downloaded on the Android and iOS. A user installs these on their smartphones to access bitcoin or other cryptocurrencies. Because of their ease of use and easy accessibility, mobile wallets are the most used ones. It is important to note that, although mobile wallets are very common, these may not be that safe as the mobile devices are always connected to the Internet.

Bitcoin had its original bitcoin wallet BitcoinQT. The very first users used it to store their bitcoins, along with access to the blockchain.

What Considerations Should I Put While Deciding on a Wallet?

Following various factors must be considered before deciding on a wallet for bitcoin or any other cryptocurrency:

1. Go for cold or offline storage, if one possesses big amount of coins.
   The examples are paper wallets or hardware-based wallets. This way, a hacker does not have access compared to storage to devices connected on the Internet always.
2. Go for software wallets when doing small transactions.
   The examples are mobile based, cloud based, website based, or from a device connected on the Internet. When a user is transacting a small amount of bitcoins, the risk of losing that amount reduces.
3. Backup the keys; create a physical copy.
   In case of loss of software wallets, the bitcoins become irretrievable unless a backup copy in cold storage is available.

Currently, there are many bitcoin wallets, with their own set of features and functionalities. Various factors to consider are listed as follows:

- Accessibility
- Amount of coins
- Anonymity
- Ease of use
- Security
- Storage media of private keys and public addresses

Remember, a bitcoin wallet does not store actual bitcoins. In fact, bitcoins are not stored anywhere. A bitcoin wallet stores the private keys to one's digital currencies, including bitcoin. A user can see the bitcoin balance using the public and private key. The private key resides in the wallet, which can be used to perform a transaction.

What Is a Good Time to Own Bitcoin?

I personally got interested in bitcoins and other cryptocurrencies as recent as 2017. While understanding the risk, I went ahead and invested in bitcoin and other digital currencies via an exchange using my credit card. I certainly missed the earliest wave, but invested in it with optimism that these digital currencies will soar higher. Again, I stuck to the philosophy of not investing more than affordability to lose it.

There is a drastic difference in the risk appetite of every single individual. One must use their own diligence, understand the risks and possible usages before deciding to own digital currencies.

How to Own Your Very First Bitcoin

The various methods to own your bitcoins are via buying, earning, or mining. Regardless, the first step is to have a bitcoin wallet. Previous topics have covered the considerations to select a wallet. Let us assume you have decided to own a physical wallet—hardware based or paper based due to safety reasons.

In case of an online wallet, a credit card can be set up for buying bitcoins or other digital currencies. In coinbase, one can set the digital currency, its amount, and frequency of transactions.

In this paragraph, I am going to share what I did to own my first digital currencies. On coinbase, I had set purchase of bitcoin, Ethereum, and litecoin for 100 U.S. dollars every Monday and the cycle repeated after three weeks. Hundred U.S. dollars' worth of bitcoin on first Monday, 100 U.S. dollars' worth of Ethereum on second Monday, and 100 U.S. dollars' worth of litecoin on third Monday, with cycle repeating after that to purchase 100 U.S. dollars' worth of bitcoin on an upcoming Monday. A confirmation e-mail confirms the transaction has taken place. I took this approach as an enthusiast to learn cryptocurrencies first hand. I do have interest in mining of other altcoins, but not bitcoin at this stage. Personally, I do not want to invest huge amount toward the hardware and software for bitcoin mining. However, I am totally open to perform mining of comparatively newer digital currencies, where I can utilize my home laptop. Also, for my online stores, I have decided to accept bitcoin as a media of exchange.

More I am getting into this world of digital currencies, more it is making me interested and create more confidence that these currencies are going to stay here, and evolve more. The blockchain has use cases wherever imaginable. This is certainly a revolution in the digital world and has the potential to change how we are going to do business in the future times. I feel glad to be part of these digital revolutions, that is, World Wide Web, dot com, and upcoming blockchain. It gives me more motivation to learn more about blockchain and cryptocurrencies from online courses so that there is enough wisdom as an end user and as a subject-matter expert on this topic.

CHAPTER 7

Bitcoin Mining

What Is Bitcoin Mining?

Bitcoin mining stands for the processing of transactions, in which the bitcoin transactions are verified so as to get added to the blockchain. The processing creates a new block that gets back-linked with the recent block in the blockchain. The blocks must get validated by a proof-of-work. Bitcoin uses HashCash toward this. Upon obtaining a block, this is broadcast to the network. This gets verified by other miners for consensus.

The participants to perform bitcoin mining are called miners. The miners get incentive to do mining. There are two parts to mining: verifying or compiling recent transactions and solving a mathematical problem. Whoever that is, a miner solves these first and gets the incentive in the form of bitcoins, and their block gets added to the blockchain. The miner incentive has two parts: transaction fees of the transactions contained in the block and newly released bitcoin. These newly released bitcoin with the successfully solved block is called a block reward.

Considering the total bitcoin supply of 21 million, a number that was set by bitcoin creator Satoshi Nakamoto, the block reward is set to get halved every 210,000 blocks as per the schedule. It is interesting to note the block reward of 50 bitcoins in 2009. As of 2018, this number has decreased to 12.5 that will further continue to decrease with more mined blocks. At the rate of bitcoin block time of 10 minutes per block, it takes about four years to have 210,000 blocks. This means that one may expect the block reward to get halved every four years. Even if it is 12.5 bitcoin for every block today, still it is a huge amount. The block reward will become zero when all the bitcoins are mined. At that time, the block reward would have halved 64 times from the creation till the end of the bitcoins. With time, mining is getting more and more difficult. With the increase in value of bitcoin over time, the value of bitcoins earned today, even if it is lesser in count, still have much higher purchase value than what it used to be. A bitcoin block is 1 MB in size.

How to Do It?

One does not need any license to do bitcoin mining. In the beginning, that is, 2009, miners used their laptops, but now those days are gone. The hardware costs are too high today to reap a reasonable benefit.

There are two methods to do bitcoin mining. Either do independently or join the mining pool. Regardless, the first step is to have a bitcoin wallet. As discussed in the earlier chapter, a hardware or paper wallet is the most secured one, compared to online or cloud-based wallets.

If one has chosen to do independent mining, it is very difficult to do on the personal laptop. Even if one gains some bitcoins, the benefits are much lower than the expenses on the electricity. Not to forget the wear and tear, hence decreased life of the hardware on personal laptop or desktop. Considering these setbacks, still if one is determined to go ahead independently, then one has to look for an application-specific integrated circuit (ASIC) miner. The ASIC miner is selected based on factors such as hashing power, efficiency, and price. It is recommended to buy an ASIC miner first-hand to avoid the high probability of burnout. In that case, a second-hand ASIC miner may burnout faster, that is, not last long enough for profits. Standard laptops for home use are not recommended to be used for mining due to high use of electricity and risk of burning the hardware.

Hashing power or hash rate is the unit of processing power of the bitcoin network. Hashing power is the power a computer or hardware uses to run and solve different hashing algorithms. The bitcoin network makes use of intensive operations related to cryptography. A hash rate of 10 Th/s means 10 trillion calculations per second. More the hashing power, more expensive is the hardware.

Efficiency is another factor of importance, as it may outweigh the benefits of bitcoin mining. A usable miner costs thousands of dollars. Electricity is the additional expense to run the hardware. Power supply adds to it. There are online calculators for bitcoin mining profit, where one inputs hash rate, bitcoin price, power consumption, and cost per power consumption unit to calculate an estimated profit per day, month, or year.

Another way of bitcoin mining is by joining a mining pool. Cloud mining allows the miners to rent hashing power. So, the first step is to choose a cloud mining service provider. Cryptocompare.com maintains a list of such service providers. The second step is to select a cloud mining package. The considerations for a package are its price and the expected return from it. One must remember that bitcoin price is very volatile; therefore, any promises or calculations based on the higher price of bitcoin may be very misleading. Generally, these mining companies require the miner to join a mining pool. The benefit of joining a mining pool is that it increases the chances of earning bitcoins. In turn, the pool charges a small percentage of the earnings.

Do I Need To Be a Technical Geek to Get Involved in It?

One must understand the underlying principles of what they are investing in. Bitcoin is not an exception. Mining needs a good deal of technical experience. A good understanding of so many concepts and process behind those is required such as bitcoin itself, how it works, wallets, wallets security, miner hardware and software, mining service providers, ability to select an efficient mining pool, and so forth.

It is interesting to note that the difficulty level adjusts itself based on the computational power. The objective is to have a constant block rate. In short, more computational power leads to a higher level of difficulty, whereas mining becomes easier if the computational power is reduced as there is a lower level of difficulty. The presence of increasing number of miners is making bitcoin mining harder, hence a need of more sophisticated equipment. The difficulty of mining gets adjusted every 2,016 blocks that corresponds to roughly every two weeks.

How to Use My Home Laptop Toward It?

In theory, a home laptop dedicated for bitcoin mining can be used. Whether it is profitable to do so is a different story altogether. A dedicated computer connected to the Internet is what anyone needs. The bitcoin mining process is very demanding in terms of processing power and electricity consumed by it. It was a common practice to use home computer for mining in its early days. However, now in 2018, bitcoin mining is rather obsolete.

Earlier in the 2009, the central processing unit (CPU) of a home computer was good enough to do bitcoin mining. On the mining of more bitcoins, it became quite difficult to do so using CPUs. Instead, graphics processing units (GPUs) gained popularity to perform the mining process. In 2013, ASICs became dominant, as these are the integrated circuits those are application specific, in this case, specifically designed for bitcoin mining. ASICs make the mining profitable compared with the use of CPUs or GPUs.

What Are the Required Software or Hardware?

Bitcoin hardware does the actual process of bitcoin mining, whereas bitcoin software is required to connect the miner with blockchain and the mining pool.

As mentioned earlier, the mining hardware has evolved from CPUs, GPUs, and then ASICs. The benefits of this evolution are better speed and lesser power consumption. The general considerations while selecting a mining hardware are the price per hash and electrical efficiency. As ASICs are designed specifically for the purpose of bitcoin mining, they become an evident option.

For the miners not interested in purchasing the hardware, they have an option to participate in the mining pool. This way, they rent the hardware on cloud subscription from the mining service providers. On that note, one can purchase simply a bitcoin cloud mining contract. Similar to altcoins, there had been numerous scams related to the mining service providers, so one needs to stay proactive by visiting bitcoin mining-related prominent forums.

The role of bitcoin software is regarding communicating information between miner and blockchain and the mining pool (if used). The software also monitors and displays various data related to hash rate, average speed, and temperature. There is no dependency on the operating systems (OS) as the mining software can run on any OS, including Windows, Mac, and Linux. There are many open-source free mining software available to perform the job.

CHAPTER 8

Learn Bitcoin Trading and Investing

What Is Bitcoin Trading?

In general, trade includes buying, selling, or exchanging commodities. Bitcoin has been being used in the similar sense. Because of the very nature of bitcoin, one may see bitcoin as a currency as well as a commodity. Apart from using bitcoin as a media of exchange, one may make profits by buying or selling bitcoin when its price in the local currency decreases or increases, respectively. The year 2017 witnessed a huge spike in the price of bitcoin. Remember the volatility of bitcoin? The past trends have seen a variation of 30 percent in its prices in a single day. Also, it is generally possible to trade bitcoin 24/7.

Due to huge variation and jumps in price, there are two segments of traders, that is, long- and short-term traders. Long-term traders hold on to bitcoins for a longer duration with hopes of its value increasing even further. Short-term traders hold on to bitcoins for a comparatively shorter duration, in a hope to encash on the daily or short-term volatility in the price of the bitcoin.

Long-term traders study the past trends similar to stocks and hold on to it. A blockchain is considered as a bigger revolution than the Internet, whose potential is not explored yet. The possible use cases of the blockchain and cryptocurrencies are expected to explode much more in value than today. That is what long-term traders hope to cash on when bitcoin value soars much higher in value.

Short-term traders count on the daily fluctuations of bitcoin price. During 2013–2017 these traders made money based on the price changes on a daily basis. The price fluctuations were very high due to the adaptation rate by the users and merchants. More and more users

and merchants are adopting bitcoin now. The adoption rate is also signi-
fied by Mrs. Watanabe. This is a term used to describe the archetypical
Japanese housewife who seeks the best use of her family's savings. Though
historically risk averse, Mrs. Watanabe became a surprisingly big player
in currency trading during the past decade to combat low interest rates in
Japan. Mrs. Watanabe also considers safe investment options.

Considering increasingly lesser fluctuations in bitcoin price and more
adoption rate with increasing acceptance by various big merchants, it
seems better time to trade or invest in bitcoin today than before. With
more knowledge of how bitcoin operates and gets used, one can reap significant benefits by bitcoin trading.

One can trade bitcoins as an exchanger. This means to identify the
local bitcoin user community. One buys the bitcoins at a little lesser price,
and then sets the threshold to sell at a little higher price. The range could
be as low as 1 percent of the normal price or willingness to trade with
higher risk appetite. Anyone can jump into this as an exchanger as it does
not need market study as such. On the other hand, a trader needs much
more financial analysis.

Are Traders Accepting Bitcoin? Which Ones?

Major traders have started accepting bitcoin as an additional method
of payment for their goods or services. The transaction fees depends on
the data size of the transaction and not on the actual amount of transaction. Regardless of the actual amount of trade, the transaction fees is the
same.

Satoshi Nakamoto, the creator of bitcoin, said in 2009:

"It might make sense just to get some in case it catches on"

And, this certainly has come true within a decade.

For the merchants, online or offline, transactions involving bitcoins
offer security. The transactions are irreversible, reducing frauds or double
spending problem. Currently, credit cards like Visa or MasterCard take a
percentage cut on transactions. With payment gateways or card processors
out of the picture, the merchants are able to keep more in their pocket.

Most of the characteristics of bitcoins, for example, security, anonymity, may be taken as advantages or disadvantages to the merchants or users, depending on the context. It is important to understand that, even if bitcoin addresses and transactions are published publicly on the blockchain, still there is a factor of anonymity as the actual identifying details of the person doing transactions are not available. However, this anonymity is lost if the details of the bitcoin address-holder are also available.

There are a variety of goods and services one may buy using bitcoins. Bitcoin can be used to buy presents, gift cards, air tickets and hotels, app stores to download movies or games, or even donate to accepting merchants. An increasing number of online merchants are accepting bitcoins as an additional method of payment. The major merchants are Expedia, CheapAir, Microsoft, and Overstock, to name a few.

Overstock.com allows major cryptocurrencies, including bitcoin, Ethereum, and litecoin for online purchases. It also holds the distinction being the first big retailer to accept bitcoins back in 2014. A user selects the bitcoin option on checkout to make the payment using bitcoins.

Expedia allows users to spend bitcoins to buy their hotel bookings. Coinbase was used to enable Expedia to do so.

Similar to eBay, Shopify offers users to have their online stores in their e-commerce platform. Shopify offers users to have bitcoin as one of their payment methods.

With bitcoins deposited as non-refundable funds, Microsoft allows users to download games, movies, or applications.

WordPress, Subway, Reddit, and Namecheap are additional merchants of reputation that accept bitcoin for their goods or services. The list continues to grow every day, hence instilling more credibility and confidence in the utility of bitcoins.

Quick response (QR) codes are becoming an increasingly popular means of payment. One can use the smartphone and wallet app by scanning the label and press the *spend* button. This way, the transaction gets completed.

As per coinmap.org, there are 12,994 venues as of July 31, 2018, that accept bitcoins as a method of payment.

As seen in the world map, the usage is not uniformly distributed. People in some countries are heavy users of bitcoins, whereas people in some countries are not into it at all, or not even heard of it. Regardless

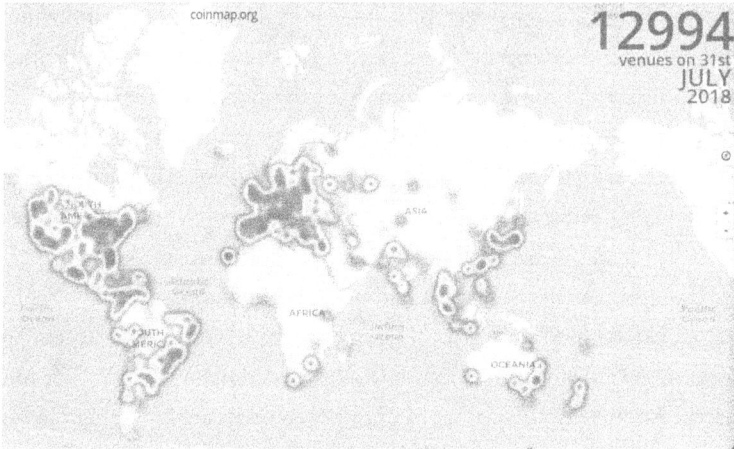

of how various countries or retailers are responding to it, it is evident that cryptocurrencies have made their stand quite prominently, bitcoin being the leader of these. Slowly and steadily, bitcoins and other digital currencies are evolving. A blockchain seems to be a big volcano in making in itself, until its use cases can be exploited.

How to Invest in Bitcoin?

There are online forums where smart investors publish their strategy that can be of use to a newcomer. Their forecasting based on their insights motivate other investors as well. Slowly, the newcomers gain more confidence and are able to use their own insights too. This way, one gets integrated into trading slowly by observing other investors who have earned profits with their strategies. Also, a long-term trader does not look at short-term gains or losses. Instead, such trader keeps the investment for a longer span of time so as to cash on the rising prices. Another strategy is to trade forex stocks with bitcoins. Worldwide news or politics affect bitcoin price in a way similar to stocks. An acceptance or ban by government, introduction of policies related to its usage affect bitcoin price. In past, the news of hacking of bitcoin exchanges affected the price in an adverse way. Bitcoin technical analysis involves formulae and statistical charts to predict the trend.

Is It Safe?

Bitcoin is evolving. More acceptance by merchants hints on its increasing credibility. However, similar to shares, it is unwise to put all eggs in a single basket. Having said that, it is not a good decision to put all money into bitcoin trading, unless someone is willing to gamble and lose all the money invested. In case of a loss, the life savings may get wiped out. One has to put extra efforts to understand bitcoin, market, changes in the prices, factors affecting the changes in prices, and use of technology enabling it. The strategies similar to those used by stock market players or forex traders can be used in bitcoin trading also. One must know when to buy or sell based on the price changes.

Will All My Earning Get Wiped Out?

In early 2018, CNBC published a news about crash of cryptocurrency market that is a prediction by a Wall Street veteran. In clear words, it is said to be a giant bubble, ready to get burst anytime. This could mean having bitcoin price fall as much as 90 percent from current levels. The surveys on the Internet show the trend in other direction. More and more credibility is coming to bitcoin because of more acceptance by major merchants.

Considering the risk and still-evolving stage of bitcoin, it is not recommended to invest life-long earnings in bitcoins. The simple thumb rule is: invest that much as you can afford to lose.

CHAPTER 9

Future of Digital Money

What Digital Money Has in Future for Us?

In this digital age, digital currency was certainly overdue, the gap of which was filled with the arrival of bitcoin. Later, many altcoins, that is, variations of free open-source bitcoin came into the digital world. Bitcoin continues to lead the world of digital currencies. There are many reputed personalities around the world who have totally dismissed bitcoin and other digital currencies. On the other hand, the adopters label it the currency of the future.

Digital currencies have one significant underlying point to eliminate the expensive third-party processors. Banks and credit card companies keep a major percentage of the actual transaction amount compared with the transaction fees in case of digital currencies. This is not in benefit to the purchaser and merchant.

Regardless of the extreme comments from various sectors, it is evident that bitcoin has made its mark in the financial sector, and in fact, gained admiration also. No doubt, bitcoin has its inherent disadvantages, still it is going strong. The new cryptocurrencies and blockchain platforms are doing fairly well. Who would have imagined that Block.one's blockchain platform called EOSIO raised 4 billion U.S. dollars in its year-long initial coin offering?

The best part of open-source code and the bitcoin community is in terms of its support to fix the defects and look into additional useful features. This way, bitcoin and other altcoins continue to evolve. The digital currencies have made their impact due to their inherent advantages discussed in earlier chapters.

Traders give great importance to the security aspect because of obvious reasons. The digital currency exchanges are not regulated as compared with their printed currency counterparts. Hackers exploit this loophole of lack of regulation to create disruption. Present regulation of the digital currencies and exchanges is likely to boost up the trust and security factors, hence increasing the value of digital currencies. This is expected to help reduce the volatility of bitcoin price the users are facing today.

Will This Surpass Conventional Currencies in Its Value?

Bitcoin shares its attributes with conventional currencies in terms of adoption rates and as a medium of exchange. Bitcoin, as a store of value, is getting termed as digital gold. It is all speculations that bitcoin will replace the conventional currencies and surpass them in its value and usage. No one has the authority to say so! Only speculations or predictions.

The current trends indicate bitcoin capturing market worth trillions of dollars in couple of years. Similar to other traditional currencies and media of exchanges, bitcoin has already made its mark as an additional method of payment.

What if Current Blocks Are All Mined? What Next?

Satoshi Nakamoto, the founder of bitcoin, had put stipulation of 21 million bitcoins, making it a finite supply. There are two paths when all the bitcoins are mined. First, the supply gets over. Second, the bitcoin community decides to update the underlying algorithm so as to have more bitcoins.

In case the finite supply reaches, bitcoin miners will not have any rewards for mining anymore. However, their source of earnings will depend solely on the transaction fees, which may be insufficient compared with present times. With technological changes, one may expect that the mining hardware will become increasingly smaller in size and lesser in costs. At the same time, an increase in the transaction fees may even out this loss of mining rewards. The miners process transactions prioritized by the transaction fees. Higher the fees, more likely the miner processes the transaction. Having said that, the higher transaction fees are expected to keep the network active and running.

Considering the principle of demand and supply, when bitcoin supply will be over, it may result into increase in its value. The creator of bitcoin saved about million bitcoins in the inception. Not to forget, many miners are having their own big share of bitcoins along with investors.

Blockchain.com has a graph depicting the bitcoins mined from the very inception till today as shown on page 60.

Approximately, 81 percent bitcoins are mined by July 2018. This means there are about 4 million more bitcoins yet to be mined. Based on the halving rewards, and increasing difficulty, last bitcoin is expected to be mined in 2140 A.D. About 20 percent of bitcoins got lost forever, simply because the miners did not expect it to reach such a high price.

Blockchain.com has various graphs related to mining information. These graphs display hash rate, hash rate distribution, difficulty, mining reserve, total transaction fees, and cost per transaction.

Will the Value Keep On Rising?

The value of a commodity increases based on various parameters, with scarcity as one of those. So, in theory, yes, the value will continue to rise. Satoshi Nakamoto, having the reserve of about a million bitcoins, may change the scenario in an unpredictable manner when the supply of bitcoins becomes more and more limited and difficult. With all the disadvantages associated with bitcoins, still it continues to rise in value. The year 2018 noticed a slow growth; in fact, a big decline in the value. However, the value seems to be stabilized by middle of the year. We must realize that digital currencies are still in the stage of infancy, so it makes even more difficult to make any conclusion with authority.

Will It Crash?

Even if the bitcoin value declined over a duration of time, it still came back! The speculation of bitcoin crash by leading banks seems to be due to their vested interests. Bitcoin is strongly about empowering an individual and eliminating the bank. The very presence of bitcoin and its increasing adoption rate have created a risk for the conventional banks or currencies. With adoption by government and presence of regulations around bitcoin, by control on scams and volatility, bitcoin is likely going to stay here in the digital era.

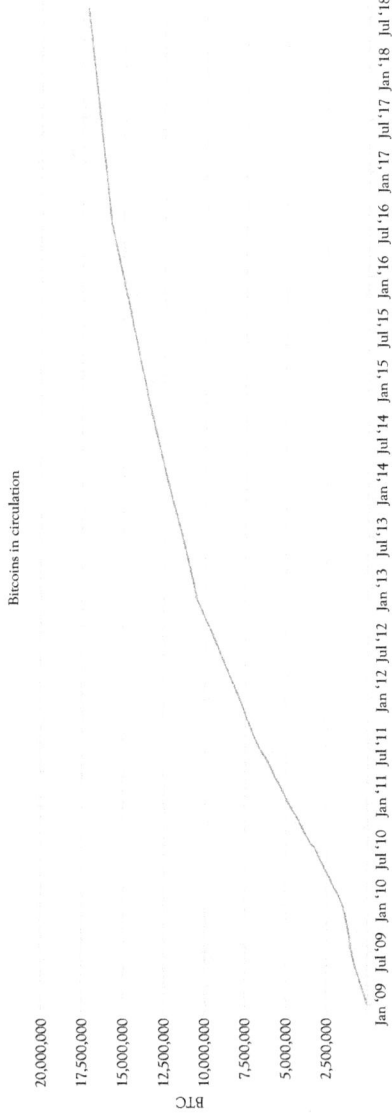

Bitcoins in circulation

Source: blockchain.info

The transactions are recorded on the blockchain and cannot simply disappear. Since 2011, there had many a few crashes in bitcoin price, but only to return stronger. In a long term, still one notices a trend where the price continues to rise despite of the devastating crashes.

What Are Forks?

Considering bitcoin or any cryptocurrency as a software, forks are a change to that software. Wikipedia defines a fork as:

- "what happens when a blockchain diverges into two potential paths forward"
- "a change in protocol" or
- a situation that "occurs when two or more blocks have the same block height"

A fork may be classified such as accidental or intentional, hard or soft, and planned or unplanned. Forking leads to more investment opportunities. There had been many bitcoin forks in the past, the list of which is generally available on the Internet.

Forking has led to creation of new altcoins, those are variants of the original bitcoin in terms of an additional feature, lack of consensus, or other factors discussed in this section. The miners race with each other to have their block to get added in the blockchain so as to get mining rewards. There have been instances where the developers disagreed on what block should get added to the blockchain. If a block was considered invalid earlier, but later found to be valid, then this is considered as a hard fork. This also includes upgrading the software. On the other hand, if a block was considered valid earlier, but has been found to be an invalid one, then this is termed as a soft fork. Based on these factors, Blockchain.com has categorized forks as follows:

- Intentional soft fork
- Unintentional soft fork
- Intentional hard fork
- Unintentional hard fork

From an investor's perspective, a fork may lead to an additional value without any additional investment. At the same time, it reduces the risk also, as the investor portfolio gets distributed over a multitude of digital currencies those were created due to forking.

What Is a Smart Contract?

Investopedia defines a smart contract as follows:

> *Smart contracts are self-executing contracts with the terms of the agreement between buyer and seller being directly written into lines of code. The code and the agreements contained therein exist across a distributed, decentralized blockchain network. Smart contracts permit trusted transactions and agreements to be carried out among disparate, anonymous parties without the need for a central authority, legal system, or external enforcement mechanism. They render transactions traceable, transparent, and irreversible.*

The term *smart contract* had been coined long before the inception of bitcoin. An American cryptographer named Nick Szabo is credited with the coining of this term. The self-executing contracts work in a similar way as digital currencies operate on the blockchain, in terms of their digital form, storage, replication, and validation on the system. Smart contracts gain importance to exchange money, property, or anything of value by eliminating the third-party middleman. Various other applications of smart contracts are toward financial derivatives, insurance premiums, execution of wills, and legal processes.

Ethereum is widely used to encode smart contracts because of its unlimited processing capability. Solidity is the language to write smart contracts. In simple words, a smart contract can be regarded as a virtual agreement for a transaction that may or may not involve money, and without involving any third party.

CHAPTER 10

How a Blockchain Is Expected to Change Various Record Keepings

Blockchain to Expand Beyond Cryptocurrencies

The two Bs, that is, bitcoin and blockchain, have been gaining attention worldwide. Though bitcoin was developed on blockchain, a blockchain is not a platform merely for cryptocurrencies only. A blockchain is a digital ledger of transactions those are publicly and permanently available to the users, without the need of an expensive third-party intervention. The transactions are secure, anonymous, and irreversible. This very nature of the blockchain makes it usable for many other purposes or commonly called use cases. Ethereum went ahead another level by creating a blockchain platform for decentralized applications (dApps).

Since the invention of Ethereum in 2015 by Vitalik Buterin, many international companies such as Deloitte, IBM, JPMorgan, and Microsoft have started experimenting with blockchain. They have identified using a blockchain in various sectors such as energy, retail, supply chain management, voting, health care, governance.

A blockchain has inherent security coupled with anonymity that is dependable. With an understanding of how a blockchain works, it can be extended to a number of use cases, something that is still in very stage of infancy. Over time, as blockchain is maturing, it may emerge as a threat for large governmental bodies due to their redundancy. Power comes back to an individual without the third-party intervention. Imagine voting without the large governmental department!

Scaling is another evolving innovation in the blockchain arena. Currently, a number of computers are involved in a network, making it slower. With a scaled blockchain, the speed of transaction processing increases without compromising the security.

With these developments in the blockchain technology, it is expected to bring phenomenal changes in how business will take place in future. A couple of decades ago, when the businesses were not on the Internet, there was a different model and accessibility. With the arrival of the Internet, the businesses went online and penetrated the international market through cyber means. Now, blockchain is on the verge of bringing another revolution of how business models will change. The direct results are reduced expenses and increased security.

Any Recordkeeping in a Secure Way

International Records Management Standard (ISO 15489-1:2016) defines a *record* as follows:

> *information created, received and maintained as evidence and as an asset by an organization or person, in pursuance of legal obligations or in the transaction of business.*

A recordkeeping system has a set of rules to manage the records. Although a blockchain is simply called a digital ledger, this is actually a distributed database. Secure, trustworthy, and permanent records and increased processing times with reduced costs are some of the basic requirements of any recordkeeping that a blockchain takes care of very well. Consider a record of house titles, registries, births, deaths, wills, legal agreements, and so on, maintained by various organizations. All these forms of records can get on the blockchain offering much more inherent benefits. There is a low possibility of having unreliable or incorrect records placed by rogue miners.

Various Other Usages in the Near Future. Uses in Financial Services, Insurance, Education, Health Care, and So On

Various other usages of a blockchain in the near future are identified as follows.

The banking, finances services, and insurance (BFSI) sector can make good use of the blockchain technology toward the next generation of their business and technological infrastructure. A blockchain enables them to capture the international market with reduced expenses and increased processing times. With global trade, the volume of international payments has been increasing every year. With blockchain, the BFSI sector would be able to reduce settlement times, and leverage further from the digital profile stored on the distributed ledger. Due to publicly available data, there is an automatic compliance with which a regulator can have on-demand access to the full historical data of a transaction.

Traders, that is, importers and exporters, use trusted financial organizations to materialize their monetary transactions. This service comes at a significant cost to the traders. In a trading activity, there are many stakeholders, such as import or export bank, customs, freight, inspection agency, regulating agency, apart from an importer and exporter. All these entities interact at some point in the trade process. This process has the characteristics of manual contracts, invoicing, inspection, miscommunication due to multiple countries involved, possible fraud, and eventually, delayed payment. With the blockchain, the trade process will have a different outlook that involves smart contract, real-time review, eliminated of intermediary banks, reduced risks, and transparency in records.

Generally, audit and compliance costs are very high. A non-compliance may result into legal consequences to an individual or organization. This is considered a very time-consuming and resource-intensive exercise. This further gets complex due to software applications not sharing information with each other at a department level. A blockchain offers real-time auditing, which also eliminates the manual errors those could creep in. Smart contracts further reduce the efforts and enable forwarding information to relevant departments. This has the potential to make the task less resource-consuming and more time and cost savings.

Voting is a potential use case of a blockchain. It may be at a political level to elect a candidate, or within an organization to gain consensus on some issue. It is generally noted that not many eligible voters vote! Organizations try to come up with various initiatives to increase the voter participation. Also, current voting processes are costly and lesser transparent. Worse is to have misleading conclusions based on voting. This resource-intensive process, if manual, becomes vulnerable to errors. With blockchain, one can expect a streamlined process for voting with more penetration to and participation by voters, smart contracts to do automatic validation, and increased transparency. Based on voting, the conclusions can be more aligned toward the betterment of the organization.

Energy is another sector where a blockchain can be used effectively, by developing a decentralized energy supply system. A smart contract to store the excessive energy produced and then matching with other parties where energy production is insufficient. A decentralized storage of transaction data with smart contracts to control the systems and ledger can directly impact how the energy sector is working today.

A blockchain can be used to streamline supply chain management. Features like real-time tracking across the globe with increased transparency has taken major retailer Walmart to partner with IBM to work on the Hyperledger blockchain. Pharmaceutical industries can make use of a blockchain to comply with regulations regarding their products.

Currently, business intelligence and analytics is an expensive and resource-intensive process used to come up with predictions or forecasts or derive conclusions based on the available data. With the predictive power in the hands of consumers directly, an organization can direct input with more accurate forecasts.

As discussed earlier, Ethereum offers a blockchain platform to build dApps. Traditional applications have their data in a centralized location or database with restricted access that is prone to failure. dApps are opposite of such traditional applications, because of which there is total elimination of single points of failure.

The Internet-of-Things (IoT) is the network of physical devices, including vehicles, home appliances, and other items in the digital form that enables these things to connect and exchange data. This is direct integration of physical world and computer applications to provide best of both the worlds in terms of efficiency improvements and reduction in errors caused by humans.

Identity management is a major use case of a blockchain. Identity records, birth certificates, passports, drivers' licenses, and marriage certificates are some of the documents for everyone. A blockchain offers the capability to encrypt the user's identity and retrieve when needed. Identity theft and fraud are major concerns in the current era. A blockchain has inherent validation and irreversibility that makes it very suitable for this purpose.

CHAPTER 11

Impact on the Traditional Banking System

Let us recap the difference of cryptocurrencies and traditional currencies also known as fiat currencies. Fiat currency is a legal tender whose value is backed by the government issuing it. There are about 200 fiat currencies around the world. Typical characteristics of a fiat currency are as follows:

- These do not have any intrinsic value, but backed by the issuing state or government.
- These can be printed or minted as needed.
- The supply is not capped.
- The banks have legal obligations toward customers.
- A fraudulent transaction can be reversed.
- No Internet connection is required to use these.
- The system is an established one for centuries. (The first fiat currency is recorded to be issued in China in 1000 AD.)
- Traditional banks act as a third party for the transactions and charge high fees to do so.

On the other hand, cryptocurrencies are almost opposite of fiat currencies with their typical characteristics as follows:

- Cryptocurrencies are not controlled by any government.
- Generally, there is a finite supply of cryptocurrency (e.g., bitcoin has a finite supply of 21 million).
- The transactions are irreversible.
- An Internet connection is required to use these.
- It is a comparatively very new system that came into existence in 2009.

- No third-party banks are required. The user pays a much smaller transaction fees than that charged by traditional banks.

Cryptocurrencies are struggling due to following reasons:

- Not many merchants accept these as a media of exchange (the number is increasing on a daily basis though).
- Every country has a different stand about their usage. Some have banned, some have put some limits around it, and some have not taken any stand yet!
- Fraudulent transactions cannot be reversed.

Is This the End of the Traditional Banking System?

The presence of cryptocurrencies will not bring an end to the traditional banking system; however, the following factors need a good consideration so as to maintain their presence:

- Governments to regulate the cryptocurrencies.
- Banks to add cryptocurrencies as an additional method of payment.
- Banks to reduce the transaction fees so as to compete with these.
- Banks to adopt the blockchain technology to gain advantage of its inherent benefits.
- Both traditional banks and cryptocurrencies to coexist for most of the world.

Can Banks Stay out of It? For How Long?

Sooner or later, the traditional banks seem to be required to adopt cryptocurrencies as an additional method of payment. Banks, like it or not, continue to dismiss cryptocurrencies due to their vested interests. The very basic principle of cryptocurrencies, especially bitcoin, is elimination of middlemen. Bitcoin claims that "It is the first decentralized peer-to-peer payment network that is powered by its users with no central authority or middlemen." This very statement poses a threat to the traditional banks. Considering the diversity of population around world and availability of the Internet or required technology, traditional banks are going to stay here for many decades yet to come.

How Will This Affect a Common User?

Users using traditional banks for their monetary transactions will be able to take the following benefits by using cryptocurrencies:

- Take control of their own transactions without paying hefty fees.
- Ability to do international transactions without involving expensive middlemen.
- Ability to do transactions 24/7.
- Anonymous transactions, that is, without any personal information associated with the transactions.
- Low transaction fees result into more savings to the user.
- The transactions are permanent or irreversible, which makes it less risky to the merchants who accept these.

Additional Readings

Etheruem.org

Bitcoin.org

Litecoin.com

Businessinsider.com

Investorpedia.com

Many more websites of various cryptocurrencies listed in the book

About the Author

Arvind Matharu is an entrepreneur with a variety of interest ranging from information technology, writing and investments. For the past few years, he developed a strong interest in cryptocurrencies. 'Learning must continue' is his personal motto. With his entrepreneurial mind-set, he was a founding partner of Dreamhouse group of companies in Canada. With a fire in his belly to continue to learn and do new things, Arvind believes in sharing his knowledge with willing readers. Apart from cryptocurrencies, his technical expertise lies in business system analysis and quality management, for which he has hands-on work experience with multi-cultural teams around the world in Canada, India, South Africa, Switzerland and United States. Arvind believes in sharing knowledge via various means with a strong interest in teaching.

Index

OTHER TITLES IN OUR FINANCE AND FINANCIAL MANAGEMENT COLLECTION

John A. Doukas, Old Dominion University, Editor

- *Escape from the Central Bank Trap: How to Escape From the $20 Trillion Monetary Expansion Unharmed* by Daniel Lacalle
- *Tips & Tricks for Excel-Based Financial Modeling: A Must for Engineers & Financial Analysts, Volume I* by M. A. Mian
- *Tips & Tricks for Excel-Based Financial Modeling: A Must for Engineers & Financial Analysts, Volume II* by M. A. Mian
- *The Anti-Bubbles: Opportunities Heading into Lehman Squared and Gold's Perfect Storm* by Diego Parrilla
- *Risk and Win!: A Simple Guide to Managing Risks in Small and Medium-Sized Organizations* by John Harvey Murray
- *Essentials of Enterprise Risk Management: Practical Concepts of ERM for General Managers* by Rick Nason and Leslie Fleming
- *Frontiers of Risk Management: Key Issues and Solutions, Volume I* by Dennis Cox
- *Frontiers of Risk Management: Key Issues and Solutions, Volume II* by Dennis Cox

Announcing the Business Expert Press Digital Library

Concise e-books business students need for classroom and research

This book can also be purchased in an e-book collection by your library as

- a one-time purchase,
- that is owned forever,
- allows for simultaneous readers,
- has no restrictions on printing, and
- can be downloaded as PDFs from within the library community.

Our digital library collections are a great solution to beat the rising cost of textbooks. E-books can be loaded into their course management systems or onto students' e-book readers. The **Business Expert Press** digital libraries are very affordable, with no obligation to buy in future years. For more information, please visit **www.businessexpertpress.com/librarians**. To set up a trial in the United States, please email **sales@businessexpertpress.com**.

www.ingramcontent.com/pod-product-compliance
Lightning Source LLC
Chambersburg PA
CBHW071116210326
41519CB00020B/6315